Lewis Carroll's Daresbury Birthplace: Idyllic but mis-placed?

An investigation into the history of the Old Parsonage, Newton-by-Daresbury, Cheshire, England.

Extent of the Daresbury Chapelry in 1844, covering nine townships. In 1824-44 the population was circa 1,700, scattered over approximately 9,000 acres. Below the tithe map compared to a modern map.

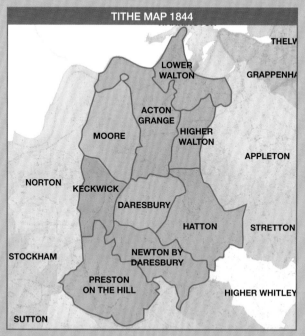

TITHE MAP 1844

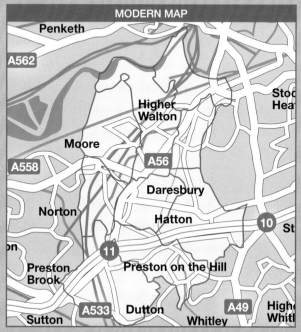

MODERN MAP

Tithe Map of 1844, from CALS (see acknowledgements).

Lewis Carroll's Daresbury Birthplace: Idyllic but Mis-placed?

An investigation by Pamela Harbutt

Lewis Carroll, real name Charles Lutwidge Dodgson, is known throughout the world as the author of *Alice's Adventures in Wonderland* and *Through the Looking-Glass*. First published in 1865 and 1871, the books have never been out of print. Each generation produces new illustrated editions and reprints of the original ones. Alice-quotes are almost a daily occurrence in the media.

What is less well known is that 'Lewis Carroll' originated in a small Cheshire village called Daresbury. After visiting Daresbury to photograph people and places he knew, Charles Dodgson described his birthplace in a poem that makes it sound idyllic:

'An island farm mid seas of corn,
Swayed by the wandering breath of morn,
The happy spot where I was born.'

From 'Faces in the Fire', 1860

For his father, the dedicated and hard-working Perpetual Curate (priest in charge) of a large and rambling parish, it is likely to have been a very different story. The Parsonage House accommodated his large family (10 children were born in Daresbury), live-in students (sometimes 6), servants and any visitors who happened to be staying – up to 25 people at times! Situated some two miles from the church and village, its inconvenient location has been a puzzle for many years.

Pamela Harbutt reveals how the Old Parsonage came to be so mis-placed, and follows its 64-year history until, it seems, it was eventually destroyed by fire. The account sheds light on the tight control of both land and development in a Cheshire village in the 1800s.

The Old Parsonage 1820-1884

Lewis Carroll was born Charles Lutwidge Dodgson, the first son and third child of Reverend Charles Dodgson, priest in charge of the parish of Daresbury in north-west Cheshire. He was born in the parsonage in 1832, and so were nine of his ten brothers and sisters. The house was built by the previous incumbent, Robert Fletcher, in 1819-20 and survived only sixty-four years, until 1884. The only remaining pictures of it were taken by Lewis Carroll in autumn 1859 or spring 1860, shortly after he had taken up the new art of photography, when he paid a visit to the place where he was born.

The parish was under the authority of the Dean and Chapter of Christ Church, a college of Oxford University, where a fascinating archive of records is held. Daresbury was a 'chapelry' within the parish of Runcorn. It had its own minister (known as a 'perpetual curate', rather than a vicar) appointed by the college, who was responsible for ten individual townships. He received an allowance or 'living' from the college, the income from the Glebe Farm (which was on church land) and some additional income from the small tithes (a form of local tax on produce). Until 1820 no accommodation was provided.

All Saints, Daresbury, from the south where the new vicarage now stands. Taken before rebuilding in 1870-1872. The old tower remains and would be recognised by earlier clergy. Moore and Daresbury Heritage Group.

A fund is established

It can be seen from the records that some incumbents had more than one parish and chose to live elsewhere and put in an assistant curate to carry out the day-to-day duties in Daresbury. These young men would have to rent somewhere to live, not a satisfactory situation, although quite common at the time.

In 1778, Reverend Joseph Blackburn (then incumbent of Daresbury) wrote to the Dean and Chapter of Christ Church to inform them that he was leaving his lease of the Newton and Hatton cow tithes (a particular local tax) to his successor.[1] His purpose was 'as a motive to promote a subscription for building a house for the Minister of Daresbury in some convenient part of the parish of Daresbury'. When he died, his estate was inherited by his nephew, still under age. The parish went to the Reverend Joseph Scott in 1787.

Mr Scott was the person mainly responsible for the building of the Daresbury parsonage. He made it his mission and there are many letters on the subject in the Christ Church Archives.

Soon after he took office as Perpetual Curate of Daresbury Chapelry, money from Queen Anne's Bounty (a fund that derived from church funds but was administered by the Crown) was used to purchase extra land for the church; £150 worth of timber was sold, the proceeds being invested by the Dean and Chapter to accumulate for the building of a house for the incumbent of Daresbury.[2] Mr Scott approached the Bishop of Chester in 1791 for a further sum of 'Bounty' money but was refused, as the living of Daresbury was worth over £60 per annum.[3]

Twenty years later he wrote to Christ Church, saying that he had viewed the trees on the estate belonging to the Chapel, and that it was time for another timber sale, and that 'Revd [George] Heron offers to auction it with some of his own'.[4] The Bishop, he added, had approved the sale, on condition that the money was transmitted to Christ Church for investment in the house fund.

'You Gentlemen may have some influence'

The following spring (1809), Mr Scott wrote to the Dean and Chapter again, saying that, he proposed to visit his parish in the Midsummer vacation (he was living in Newport on the Isle of Wight, with an assistant curate in Daresbury), and would 'look out for a suitable situation to erect a house upon for the use of the Chapel, as soon as the fund is sufficient for the purpose.'[5] Although he is not very hopeful about Mr Heron, 'who is the proprietor of the whole of the lands on the township of Daresbury', he says 'There are some beautiful situations at a very small distance from the Chapel, belonging to Sir Richard Brooke, with whom you Gentlemen may probably have influence enough to prevail upon him to accommodate the Chapelry with a few acres of Land, as I understand he holds a considerable quantity of tithes under lease from the College.' He adds: 'I have in the funds and in my hands between £300 and £400 which I have received from the Cow Tithe of the Parish, left by will to the chapel by the late incumbent, but as the validity of the will is doubtful from some error in it, I should not feel myself inclined to lay it out in the building of a house unless indemnified by the College.'

His search for land must have been in vain, as in June 1812 he wrote in desperation, asking for the help of the Dean and Chapter in persuading the local gentry to offer a site:

'I am Curate of the Chapelry of Daresbury Co[unty] Chester, the parish is very extensive and populous, there is no parsonage house, which in so large a parish must be very needsome, and essential to the interests of the parishioners as well as the Curate.

'I have been looking out for a situation for the erection of one. I have applied to the Revd Mr Heron, who is not disposed to accommodate. I have likewise applied to Sir Richd Brooke of Norton, who has several townships in the Chapelry, and one adjoining to Daresbury, distant not more than four hundred yards from the Chapel, he likewise has refused, thinking it would disfigure his township, tho the piece of land solicited, is at the very extremity of the Township. I have thought proper to state the circumstances to you, Gentlemen, hoping you may have more interest with Sir Richd.'[6]

The fund is assured

Nearly four years later, in March 1816, the Dean and Chapter of Christ Church received yet another letter on the subject from Mr Scott.[7] The nephew of his predecessor had now come of age and did not wish to go against his uncle's wishes. The money from the Easter Roll (the Cow Tithes) was therefore assured and Mr Scott asked the Dean and Chapter, once again, to try and prevail upon Sir Richard Brooke to make some land available. Writing from Newport, he said he would go to Daresbury in the summer to see if any land was available in one of the other townships.

Negotiation and compromise

The following month, there was a Letter from General Heron (nephew of Reverend George Heron) to Dr Charles Hall, Christ Church.[8] He stated that Daresbury parish consisted of ten hamlets and that 'it has been the great object of my Father and myself to obtain the exclusive possession of the hamlet of Daresbury, which after many years, with great Difficulty and much Expense, I have at last accomplished.' He therefore refused to part with land for a parsonage and suggested trying another hamlet in the parish. Similarly unhelpful was a letter from Sir Richard Brooke, who simply lamented his inability to part with land at Acton Grange and pointed out that he owned none in Daresbury township.[9]

Mr Scott must have kept his promise to pursue a site in the summer as he wrote excitedly on 27th October that General Heron had agreed to make a site available for the parsonage house in Hatton, either in exchange for glebe belonging to the Chapelry, or by purchase. The site was a good one, on the turnpike road and there was no possibility of anything nearer.[10] A second letter, a month later, said that General Heron wanted the exchange to take place immediately. Mr Blackburn was ready to present the Easter Roll money to the Chapelry and that would procure the grant from Queen Anne's Bounty.[11] This was November 1816. He must have believed that the end was finally in sight!

He received a reply within a few days: Christ Church preferred that, rather than exchange any of the Glebe Farm land, four or five acres should be purchased. There was plenty of money available, some £700 having been invested at 3%, in addition to the money from the Easter Rolls [the Cow Tithes], and that the Rule of Queen Anne's Bounty was to advance £300 for each £200. The Dean and Chapter also required plans and specifications for a house.[12] Mr Scott replied on 20th December 1816, saying he was just about to carry out the exchange with General Heron, whose uncle, Reverend Heron, had recommended Thomas Wedge as the surveyor to carry out the valuation.[13]

Disappointment ...

In a one-sided correspondence, some of the important facts are missing. The next relevant document in the archives is a copy of Mr Wedge's valuation report, dated 26th April 1817.[14] Poor Mr Scott! Mr Wedge was not inclined to agree to the proposed exchange: the land at Hatton was wet and cold and was to be exchanged for some of the best of the glebe land. He would prefer a good house to be built on the glebe, which would increase its value and enable the incumbent to manage the land to the best advantage. In some frustration, Mr Scott replied on the same day.

He stated that: '... the piece of land on which Mr Wedge recommends to build, is by far the best of the whole farm. There is a valuable meadow adjoining this, the whole or a part of this must likewise be taken for the life of the Glebe house, which of course will very much reduce the value of the Farm.'

... And a new opportunity

However, he had another suggestion – a new opportunity had come up.

'... We have an opportunity of adding as much to the farm as we are taking away from it for the accommodation of the Glebe House. There are now upon Sale three pieces of land in the very centre of our estate, one of them a very valuable meadow, which I am told may be purchased upon reasonable terms...

'Certainly Gentlemen, when we have received Mr Blackburn's bequest, with what money may be expected from Queen Anne's Bounty, and what we have in the Funds from the Sale of timber, we shall have abundantly sufficient both to purchase this Land and to build a Glebe house and offices.'[15]

There is no further mention of these three pieces of land and by 23rd October 1818, Reverend Joseph Scott, after some thirty years as incumbent of the parish of Daresbury, was dead.

The respectable Curate

On this date, there was an application from his assistant curate, the Reverend Robert Fletcher, to be appointed in his place:

'I have been Mr Scott's Curate of Daresbury for a period of nearly fourteen years [ie since 1804] and always resident in the Chapelry. The Curacy in point of stipend has been of little value and I have in a great measure supported my family by admitting pupils into my house, yet the Curacy has added to the respectability of my situation and is now an object of solicitude to me ... I can only presume to ask this favour on the supposition that the living may be refused by those who have the first claim – and then my long services and my being stationed in the Parish where a stranger could hardly procure a comfortable lodging, may perhaps weigh with you in the disposal of it. With respect to character and principles, I would refer to the Gentlemen of the Parish and neighbouring Clergy. In the mean time the duties of the Church shall be duly performed ...'[16]

Six weeks later he wrote again, giving a detailed description of the Chapelry, its townships and the value of the Glebe Farm (which he had been renting for the last year) and the tithes. He gave the population of the parish as '1719 souls' according to the latest census. He explained that the Chapelry of Daresbury consisted of ten townships: Daresbury, Hatton, Newton, Preston, Keckwick, Acton Grange, Over Walton, Lower Walton, Moore, and Thelwall.

Through these ten townships a tithe was collected (called the Cow Tithe), the amount annually after expense of collecting was deducted was £20 to £21. The incumbent Minister never derived any benefit from this; it was to accumulate for the purpose of building a parsonage house. He concluded: 'The above is a just statement of the Profits accruing to the late Mr Scott as Incumbent Minister of Daresbury and Lessee of the Corn and Hay tithe of the township of Newton and of the Hay tithe of the township of Hatton under Christ Church.'[17]

Why not build on the Glebe land?

In March 1819, Robert Fletcher brought up the subject of building a parsonage in the same letter that acknowledged 'the favour of my Nomination to the Curacy of Daresbury'. He pointed out the disadvantages, but admitted that:

'The church land appears to be the only Situation at present attainable. One field is pleasantly situated for the purpose of building, the distance (about two miles) from the Church and the state of the road leading to it excepted – but these are inconveniences which might be obviated, admitting that the road were mended and the Curate would afford the keeping of a horse. Under such circumstances I should be very glad to fix my abode there in a house sufficiently commodious for my family and a few Pupils. In building a house it would be well to have in view the probable wish of future curates to have accommodation for the reception of a few Boys, both as affording increased means of supporting a family and laudable employment of time in a situation which will confine a man almost to the society of his own fire side.'[18] He is aware of the remote situation but has taken it into account.

No milk for money!

In April, another site was considered; it was only about a mile from the church but four people's interests were involved. Mr Fletcher said it was imperative that the Curate should be able to have a horse and two cows, or possibly three cows, because: 'The farmer's unwillingness to rob his Cheese tub renders it impossible to procure milk for money'!

He had given a plan for a house to someone to value and expected to hear in the week.[19]

Mr Blackburn needs proof

On 29th April, the Archives show that Mr John Blackburn had been approached to forward the money left to him by Reverend Joseph Blackburn, in trust for the house-fund. He wrote to the Dean and Chapter: 'You must be aware that presenting a sum of £600 to a society with whom I have no connexion, for the benefit of a parish in which I have no interest can only proceed from a wish to carry into effect the will of a person to whom I am so much indebted, as I am to my late uncle.' He will forward the money, but only when he sees 'a wish for this purpose evinced by the acts of those interested' and not before![20]

A plan is drawn up

On 7th June 1819, Reverend Robert Fletcher wrote to the Dean and Chapter in great excitement:

'I shall this day forward by the Coach a plan of specification and estimate of the house proposed to be built for the residence of the Minister of Daresbury. I propose to erect it on the Glebe land which is pleasantly situated in the Township of Newton and only objectionable in point of distance from the Church.' He doubted if a satisfactory title could have been exchanged on the site he was previously considering and although one was also available at £2,000, it was still at two miles distance. He was almost carried away by enthusiasm!

'If the plan and estimate meet the approbation of the Dean and Chapter and of the Committee for Queen Anne's Bounty there is yet time to undertake and accomplish the building this Summer. By making Bricks on the premises there would be a saving of £60 or £70 – or I could purchase bricks and proceed immediately to build. I have ascertained the nature of the clay and find it suitable for the purpose of making it into brick at this late period; but no farther {sic} delay should take place and to be ready for either plan I shall begin to cast the clay tomorrow, the expense of which I shall defray if the clay is not wanted.'[21]

Getting the funds in place

Two weeks later the Treasurer of Christ Church wrote to Mr J Blackburn, asking for the £600 from his uncle's covenant[22] and, finally on 1st July 1819, he wrote to the Treasurer of the Bounty Office that they were about to advance three sums of £200 each to him 'in order to obtain augmentation of £300 for each from the Parliamentary Grant, the benefaction being for the living of Daresbury'.[23] On September 2nd, he wrote again: 'I hope that the answers of the Diocese to the usual queries will secure the full advance from the Parl. Grant in aid of this desirable object which the Dean and Chapter have long been very anxious to accomplish.' He points out that he finds 'that the work is already far advanced' and begs 'the favour of an early answer.'[24]

While the bureaucratic wheels are turning ...

Bundled with the plans for the Parsonage House in Chester Record Office is a fascinating series of letters that throw light on the delay in receiving the money.[25] First, there is a copy of the letter just mentioned. The reply does not come until 8th September and states that the delay is due to 'some correspondence between Mr Burn [Treasurer] and the Incumbt. respecting the population', that the papers will be submitted to the Governors at the first opportunity – 'but I apprehend they will be of opinion that it was premature to begin building the house before the plans had been laid before them for their approbation ... and before they had approved the Living as proper for augmentation by them.'[26] It sounds as though both Christ Church and Mr Fletcher are being thoroughly ticked off.

Finally, the approval of plans for the Parsonage was sent to Christ Church on 5th November 1819.[27] This was the first step. There were some printed papers enclosed, to inform the incumbent on how he should proceed. He was to send to the Bounty Office:

'A Plan, Specification and Estimate of the Expense of building or rebuilding such Parsonage House and suitable Erections, to be verified by the affidavit of a Surveyor ; and an undertaking on the Part of the Surveyor, or some respectable Workman, to do the Work in a good substantial and workmanlike manner, and according to the Plan and Estimate, for the sum stipulated.' The good news was passed on to Mr Fletcher on 18th.[28]

... The builder is already at work

Mr Robert Fletcher, meanwhile, had already put the matter in hand. The Estimate and Specification for the building of Daresbury Parsonage, now in the Cheshire Record Office, is dated 15th July 1819.[29] It is signed by Robert Fletcher and the builder he had contracted to do the work: Thomas Haddock. The sum agreed was £1,275..0s..0d.

Approval, but no money yet!

Mr Fletcher wrote to Christ Church on 18th November, replying to their letter of the same date. He was most disappointed at the delay in receiving the Queen Anne's Bounty money and in fact, he had been authorised by Mr Morrell, the Christ Church solicitor, to contract for the building of the Parsonage House. He had stipulated 'as suggested by Mr Morrell that one half of the Estimate should be paid at Michaelmas last and the other half on the completion of the building.' The house was now 'in a considerable state of forwardness' and they would, he said, 'be sensible of the unpleasant situation in which the unavoidable nonfulfilment of the contract on my part has placed me.' He went on to say that as the builder was 'urgent for the payment of the money due at Michaelmas £637..10s..0d', he had advanced £300 from his private resources and 'any farther {sic} advance would be extremely inconvenient'. He asked if the money could not be paid from 'some other source ... Or if I could at present even be favored with the £337..10s in the balance on the Michaelmas payment it would release me from the importunity and expedite the finisheing {sic} of the house.'

He was adding to the plan 'a Gig house with a Room over it useful as a Laundry or for many other purposes, the expense of which, if the funds for improving the living of Daresbury will not admit, must fall upon myself.'[30] (It is interesting to note that this has been handwritten onto the plans, upside down in the top margin, and signed R.Fletcher, see page 18).

What the builder said

Perhaps the most interesting letter in the Christ Church archive is from the builder himself, Mr Thomas Haddock. It was enclosed with one from Mr Fletcher, sent to Mr Robert Morrell the Christ Church solicitor.

'Revd Robt Fletcher of Dasbury as given me your letter of the 18th in which you request me to State the amount of Money already laid out in the Building of his House, on the Church Land. That is to say a House for the Curate of Dasbury. And my demand against him or the Govnors is as follows. There is now Expended on the Premises from Ten to Eleven hundred pounds. My agreement with Mr Fletcher was to Receive on the 30th day of September £800..0s..0d which is now very much wanted.'[31]

This seems to have produced the desired effect because a letter to Mr Fletcher, dated 26th November, enclosed 'a draft for 337.10' and hoped that 'no farther {sic} difficulties [would] occur'. The writer presumed (wrongly, it appears) that he would have 'before this time transmitted the proper documents to be laid before the Govrs of Q A's Bounty' and sent him a reminder of what was required.[32] He replied a few days later, not confirming that he had sent the papers, but pointing out that he had already had to give the builder another £100 and 'the favour of another remittance from you as soon as convenient [would] be very acceptable'.[33]

The Governors want the boxes ticked

On 14th December Robert Fletcher wrote direct to the Bounty Office, enclosing (at last) the 'Plan Estimate and Specification of a House and Buildings now erecting for the Minister of the Parochial Chapel of Daresbury ... on the Glebe Lands belonging to the said Chapel.' He continued that as he had: 'almost daily inspected progress of the building' he could assure them 'it is erected in a firm substantial manner and will be a permanent benefit to the incumbents of Daresbury.'[34] The reply he received was somewhat cold. He was informed that his documents were received too late – and anyway there was no 'Affidavit to verify the Estimate of Expense of the Building, nor any undertaking on the part of your Surveyor as to the respectable Workman to do the Work in a good substantial and Workmanlike manner.'[35]

The next set of documents, dated 12th February 1820, consists of a letter from Mr Fletcher, an affidavit from his builder and another from Edward Alcock, surveyor, stating that he has inspected the building and that it is indeed being built in a workmanlike manner. Although it is signed: 'sworn before me this 12th day of February 1820 [signature]', the receiver has

The frontage of the Parsonage House, as photographed by
Lewis Carroll in 1859. SSPL/National Media Museum, Bradford.

pencilled on 'not stated to be a magistrate'.[36] Box ticking is nothing new! In another letter and affidavit from the surveyor, dated 3rd April, Mr Fletcher states: 'I now take the liberty to enclose an affidavit certifying that the Parsonage House and Outbuildings erected on the Glebe Land of Daresbury are in a finished state and worth the stipulated sum of £1275 the payment of which by Agreement is now due.'[37]

He wrote again on 28th April, asking the Bounty Treasurer to 'excuse the liberty I take in reminding you of the obligation I am under to pay the estimated sum for building a Parsonage House' which he hopes 'to occupy in a week or two'.[38] The reply he received on 8th May came from the Bounty Office's solicitor in Gray's Inn. The Governors of Queen Anne's Bounty had 'felt [themselves] in some difficulty' in paying the sum requested and had asked their Counsel's opinion. However, he had just given it. 'He thinks the Governors may properly pay the money and his opinion will be read at the next Board held by them, after which you will no doubt hear from Mr Burn [Treasurer to the Governors].'[39]

The builder is pushing for payment

But by 19th June, the Parson had still not received the money! He was certainly being punished for his presumption in beginning to build before the Bounty Office had given its hard-won approval, even though the work had been agreed by Christ Church. This time Mr Fletcher wrote to Christ Church, admitting that he was being pressed by the builder, who was 'urgent for the payment of the specified Sum of £1275', towards which he had already paid £406. He had also promised to pay another £306 by 9th August.[40]

The exact date when payment was finally made is not given but the 'Summary', enclosed on a scrap of paper, says that £600 was advanced from Christ Church and £900 received from the office of Queen Anne's Bounty, making a total of £1500.[41]

The Parsonage House

And so, a Parsonage was finally built for the Perpetual Curate of Daresbury. It was built largely in common brick, presumably made locally as Mr Fletcher had promised, the frontage built in Flemish Bond, a decorative pattern giving strong, two-brick deep walls. The red sandstone flags that floored the shippon [cow shed] and stable were quarried locally, in Daresbury Delph, where the Daresbury Expressway now runs. The roof was of Welsh slate.

From the 'Estimate and Specification for the building of Daresbury Parsonage',[42] we can conjure up the house in some detail. The photos that Lewis Carroll took some forty years later suggest a fine Georgian property and the Ordnance Survey map from 1877[43] shows an extensive garden with pathways.

Lobby and upper floor

The Specification describes an eight-panelled front door with a fanlight over, and the stonemasons are asked to add a 'Plinth course to front of House, 2 feet wide and 6 inches thick' which can be seen in the photo. Two steps were to lead up to the door, which would have a sanded wooden column to each side of it. It was to have a 'lackerd Knob … and iron rapper' and would open onto a lobby paved with 'polish'd random flags' and a staircase built 'with Mahogany handrail and Iron Newall [post]' leading up to the seven 'chambers' or bedrooms, three of the doors with '6 inch iron rimb Locks' and 'spring latches to all the remainder'. The chamber floors were to be covered with 'inch deal [pine] boards punched and puttied' and the walls and ceilings were to have '2 coat Stuco work' (stucco, a kind of plaster) and sash windows with iron pullies. This upper floor was to be 9 feet (2.77m) in height.

Ground floor

On the ground floor, the main rooms at the front are the dining room (called 'sitting room' on the plan) and the parlour. They are to have three coats of stucco plaster applied to walls and ceilings and a 'neat plain cornice in each' and both are to have deal board floors and 'large polish'd hearths'. Their windows are to have 'brass axle pullies' to open them. The other downstairs rooms are, on the left, the principal kitchen and back kitchen, giving onto the yard, and on the right the two pantries (one lockable) and extending behind them along the yard, the study and the schoolroom. These rooms are to have 'unpolished hearths and shutters to the windows'. The kitchens and pantries will have 'common flags' on their floors. All the downstairs rooms are to be 10 feet (3 metres) high and every fireplace is to have a 'neat white stone chimney piece'.

Cellars and outbuildings

There are to be two cellars underneath the two kitchens, rendered and with '2 coats of white wash'. They will have 'lattis windows with Iron stantions [stanchions, vertical bars] and shutters inside' and their doors

Ground floor plan for the Parsonage House

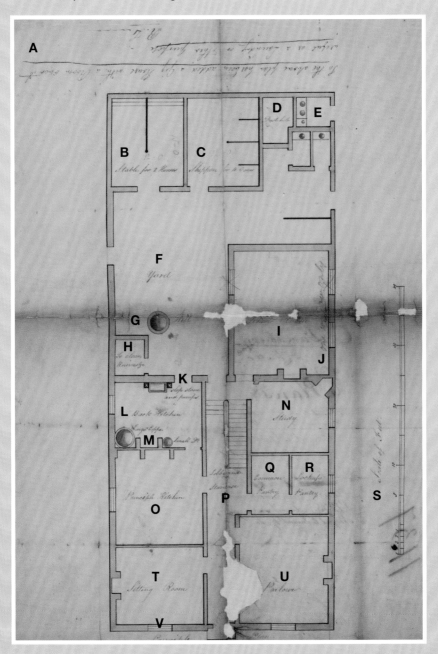

Principle {sic} Plan

First floor and cellar plans for the Parsonage House

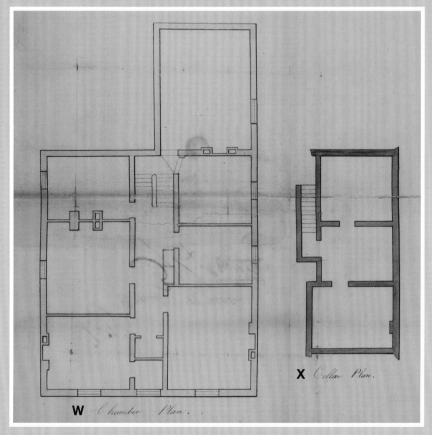

Chamber Plan and Cellar Plan

A 'To the above plan has been added a Gig House with a Room over it useful as a Laundry or other purpose, R. Fletcher'

B Stable for 2 horses

C Shippon for 4 cows

D Dust hole

E 'Necessaries', WCs

F Yard

G Well

H To clean knives &c

I School Room

J One window only

K Slop stone & pumps

L Back Kitchen

M Large Copper, Small Copper

N Study

O Principle {sic} Kitchen

P Lobby & Staircase

Q Common Pantry

R Lockable Pantry

S Scale of feet

T Sitting Room, Dining Room in 'Specification'

U Parlour

V Principle {sic} plan

W Chamber Plan

X Cellar Plan

are to have '2 stock locks'. 'They will be 6'6" from Topside of floor to underside of Joice [joist]'.

Out in the yard are a well and a large cistern: '8 feet [2.46 metres] long, 4½ feet [1.38 metres] deep, and 5 feet [1.54 metres] wide, to receive the rain water'. The well and the cistern will have a pump each. At the end of the yard, with its walls 7 feet [2.15 metres] high, will be the 'shippon' or cowshed for 4 cows, the stable and 'the necessaries' (toilet facilities). Even the size of the stall in the manger is specified: '6ft heigh and 4ft and 7½ ft long'. Water will be carried to the back kitchen 'with two inch patent [lead] pipe and wood case' and the different weights of lead for cornices, spouts and gutters are specified.

Trial excavation only

The limited trial excavation of the site carried out in 1990 (see below) was only able to confirm 'an accurate ground plan of part of the house, using the lines of the robber trenches as a guide to the original foundation trenches' and the site of the well-head, which remains. Very little of the original brickwork was found in place, although it was suggested that further excavation in the area of the cellars might reveal their original brick and flag floors.[44]

The Dodgsons come to Daresbury

ARCHDEACON DODGSON AS A YOUNG MAN.

Left: Photograph of Archdeacon Dodgson, Lewis Carroll's father, as a young man. From *The Life and Letters of Lewis Carroll,* by S.D. Collingwood, 1898. Centre and right: Letter from Reverend Charles Dodgson to Christ Church in 1832. From Christ Church Archives, Runcorn and Daresbury.

When, in 1827, Robert Fletcher died and Reverend Charles Dodgson, aged 27, arrived in Daresbury with his young wife Frances, this was the seven-year-old house they moved into. Their eldest daughter was born in 1828, another in 1830 and when Mr Dodgson wrote to Dr John Bull at Christ Church on 23rd January 1832, the birth of their third child was imminent. Charles was born just four days later. The letter made no complaints about the Parsonage; Mr Dodgson was discussing the Potato Tithe and seeking permission to fell more timber so that he could be reimbursed for expenses he had had in repairing the Glebe Farmhouse and manuring the fields, ready for re-letting. He did however point out his financial worries: 'I already begin to experience the anxieties incidental to my situation, having at this moment two vacancies for Pupils unfilled.'[45] He was permitted to sell the timber, as long as whatever was not needed for repair was invested for the benefit of the living.[46]

What the census tells us

Left: Mary Cliff is listed as a 15 year old washerwoman in 1841 census. Lewis Carroll's photo of her 1859. SSPL / National Media Museum, Bradford. Centre: Photo of Morphany (modern spelling) Hall, since demolished, postcard. Moore and Daresbury Heritage Group. Right: 1831 map showing proximity of Hall to Parsonage. Bryant, CALS, ref M5.2.

The census of 1841 shows, at the Parsonage: 24 people (3 of them students, one of them Mrs Dodgson's sister, Aunt Lucy Lutwidge). The ninth little Dodgson was born in that year. Also listed were 10 other people including 2 washerwomen, 2 agricultural labourers and a shoemaker's apprentice, as well as a little girl of 6, probably daughter of one of the servants.[47] There could easily have been 25-30 people to be fed daily! Sometimes included were the children from Morphany Hall, the nearest farm to the Parsonage. Reverend Charles Dodgson remained in this position for sixteen years in all and then in 1843 the Dodgson family moved on to a far more comfortable home in north-east Yorkshire. As Rector of the parish of Croft-on-Tees, Mr Dodgson had a large house and garden and a much improved and secure income.

Reverend Fawkes winters elsewhere

However, the next incumbent chose not to live in the Parsonage. A letter from Christ Church on 5th December 1844 lamented the fact that Reverend John Bracker Fawkes was not living in the parish and suggested that if he had no chance of returning, he should resign.[48] Mr Fawkes replied from Ventnor, Isle of Wight, that his health was improving and that he would return in the spring. There had obviously been discussion about the site of the Parsonage House, as he wrote that he did not think there was any more suitable house to be had at present. He continued: 'It would of course be desirable in many respects, that this residence of the Incumbent should be near the Church' and promised to let the Dean and Chapter know if one should become available.[49] After less than forty years, the location of the house was already causing problems.

Left: Detail from Mr Fawkes' letter from the Isle of Wight. Note that this is a 'crossed letter' – it was cheaper to send as one page. Christ Church Archives, Runcorn and Daresbury.

At this time the tithe maps were being drawn up and Mr Fawkes is shown as 'owner' of the church lands and 'occupier' of the Parochial Chapel and Yard and Parsonage House and Gardens.[50] In the Census of 1851, he is shown living as the 'lodger' of Elizabeth Morris (a widow), in the village itself.[51] The next incumbent confirms this, saying that his predecessor 'left the Parsonage shut up and took no thought or care of it.'[52]

'Unfortunately placed'

By January 1857, the inhabitants of the parish were petitioning the Dean and Chapter for an increase in the value of the living. They described the Parsonage House as 'unfortunately placed in a remote corner of the least populous part of the Chapelry at an inconvenient distance from the villages where the largest number of the Inhabitants reside: viz. From Lower Walton

Top: The Old Parsonage, from the side, photo by Lewis Carroll in 1859/60. The building to the right appears to be the 'carriage house', formerly known as the 'gig house'. SSPL / National Media Museum, Bradford. Below: Published by Bryant, CRO, ref M5.2.

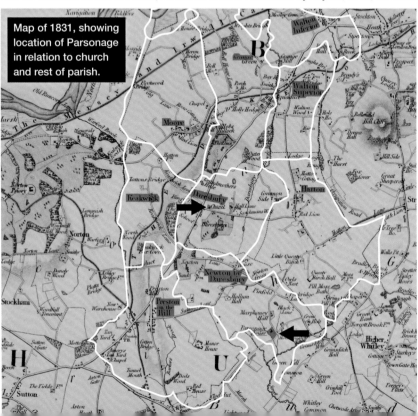

Map of 1831, showing location of Parsonage in relation to church and rest of parish.

Possible (walking) route from Daresbury church to
the Parsonage House, based on tithe map of 1844.
Cheshire Archives and Local History.

upwards of 4 miles, from Moore 4 miles, from Higher Walton 3 miles, from Preston 2 miles, from Hatton 2 miles and from the Church 2 miles.' Since this entailed 'increased labour and expense in the discharge of his duties' on the incumbent, they asked the Dean and Chapter to consider whether there was any way in which they could increase the living from the tithes of the Chapelry, which would normally come to them.[53]

What the Curate heard!

The petition was signed by a number of leading landowners and seems to have been successful. On 1st August 1857 Daresbury's new incumbent, the Reverend William H Spencer, asked from whom he should draw the £9 Parliamentary grant to Daresbury and also 'the augmentation of £30 from Christ Church'. The Parsonage House, he reported, was 'large and in a fair state of repair', but 'much is built very slightly, especially the rooms added by Dodgson'. (He does not record which rooms the latter built; perhaps, because of his many children, he was responsible for redividing the rooms on the first floor, as described in the report of 1884, see below.)

His next assertion suggests that village gossip has created a legend. Mr Spencer has heard that Reverend Robert Fletcher built the house on its present site in order to be out of the way! The reason for this, he has heard, is that Fletcher lost his reputation among the parishioners by drinking and by marrying his servant. The church services on Sunday morning 'were sometimes omitted for lack of a congregation', and Fletcher used 'to sit in the tap room of the Public House'.[54]

It is true that Mr Fletcher was damned by omission by his Churchwarden. When the latter delivered his tribute to Reverend Charles Dodgson (his successor), on his move to Croft, he stated that, before Mr Dodgson came: '… no Sunday-school existed, no week-day Lectures were given – no efficient visitations to the sick and poorer classes took place and the Sunday congregations in our Church were lamentably small.'[55] But the site of the Parsonage, as shown above, is surely the result of the refusal by any of the local landowners to give up any land that was more conveniently situated.

Mr Spencer feels 'as useless as if I was not resident'

Three months later, Mr Spencer wrote again to Dr John Bull at Christ Church, having failed to see him on a visit to Oxford. He wrote a long letter, describing his predicament in great detail.

'The Parsonage house, which is two miles from the Church and School is situated on the very outskirts of the parish – in a lane, which branches off from another lane – a mile and a half from the highroad and is as far removed as it properly could be from the many townships which comprise the parish. And what is still worse allows no way to them except across the fields unless I go a long way round – the difference being two or three miles.' And it will be worse in the winter. Even in the summer it prevents him from holding an evening service. It makes it very difficult for him to attend the school, 'which is in a most inefficient and neglected state' and it impedes his care of the sick, 'except in most urgent cases'. In short: 'the position of the house cripples the usefulness and benefit of a resident minister.' On a personal note, he says that 'the difficulty of getting provisions or a parcel or a letter are not trifling domestic inconveniences'.

He has a solution: 'If the house was in Daresbury all these difficulties would be at once remedied. It would be on the high road, close to the Church and schools, and in the centre of the townships – with good roads leading to each.' However, having found that the local landowner was not interested and hearing from the Land Agent in Warrington that 'no-one would buy the house, because of its position', he suggests that the only way to improve matters is 'to pull it down and rebuild it in Daresbury'.

He concludes: 'It is a grief to me that these things are so – and a most serious misfortune to the parish if they are to be allowed to continue. I am anxious to fulfil my duties but I feel myself as useless as if I was not resident.'[56] This only forty-seven years after Reverend Robert Fletcher had been so enthusiastic that he started building before receiving funds and final permission! Perhaps he really did care 'more for the glebe than the parish', as Lewis Carroll's nephew, S D Collingwood had heard.[57]

Lewis Carroll's photographs

It is just about two years after this complaining letter that the only known photos of the Old Parsonage were taken, by Charles Lutwidge Dodgson (Lewis Carroll) on a visit to Daresbury, most likely in autumn 1859.[58] He had loved his childhood home and described it in a poem written about this time as: 'An island farm mid seas of corn, Swayed by the wandering breath of morn, The happy spot where I was born.' 'Faces In The Fire', Jan 1860.

He took three views of the house, from the front, from the side and over the five-bar gate from the fields (see front cover, pages 14-15, page 23).

Left: Phoebe Thomas Bostock Irwin, landlady of The Ring O'Bells, as photographed by Lewis Carroll in 1859. SSPL / National Media Museum, Bradford. Above: Photo of the Ring O'Bells, circa 1910. Moore and Daresbury Heritage Group.

These photos show a sturdy, detached Georgian house, double-fronted, two-storey, with a semi-circular fanlight over the door and a decorative porch, just as specified in July 1819.[59] At the same time, Lewis Carroll photographed some of the people he had known in his childhood: servants, clerical acquaintances and the landlady of the Ring O'Bells.

The advowson is revalued

The next mention of the Parsonage in the Christ Church Archives comes in 1861, when a detailed valuation is logged. It seemed they had a plan. Mr Henry White, a Warrington surveyor, valued the house and buildings at £30, the 25 acres of farmland at Newton, together with 31 acres at Lower Whitley at £90 and then went on to value the tithe rent and money held for the parish by the Dean and Chapter. The final 'value of the advowson to the incumbent aged 42 [Mr Spencer]: £768..0s..0d.'[60]

Christ Church sells to local landowner

There was a reason for the valuation. In May 1861, the whole 'advowson' [the legal right to appoint or recommend a parish priest] was sold by Christ Church to Gilbert Greenall of Walton Hall, a brewer, magistrate and MP of Warrington, who often worshipped at Daresbury, for £1,000.[61] The money was to be invested, the interest being used to support small livings still in the care of Christ Church.

On 26th February 1880 the ecclesiastical parish of Daresbury (by then a smaller area) finally became independent of Christ Church.[62]

In a poor state of repair

Mr Spencer died on 16th October 1883 and it seems that the Parsonage House had been left uninhabited for some months and fell into a poor state of repair. Following the Ecclesiastical Dilapidations Act, 1871, this was something which the incumbent was 'by law or custom bound to maintain in Repair' and therefore it fell to 'the executors or administrators of Reverend William Henry Spencer the late Incumbent thereof' to pay for the work to be carried out.[63] What happened next is unclear.

Reverend Thomas Whitley was appointed to the living on 8th August 1884.[64] A survey of the work to be done was carried out for the Bishop of Chester and the report, dated 15th August 1884, gives a very detailed description, room by room, of all repairing, refitting, relaying and making good required.

Floors are to be taken up and 'resquared and relaid', plastering is to be 'thoroughly repaired', grates are to be 'reset', window sashes are to be 'rehung', rotten floorboards are to be removed and replaced and 'door and window fastenings throughout to be examined and left perfect and keys provided to all locks where requisite.' The stable floor is to be relaid with 'proper channel stones' and the 'loft over the stable' needs repairs to the floor and door.

Left and centre: Introduction and Particulars of Repairs to the Dilapidations report on the Parsonage House, August 1884. CALS. Right: Well-head at the Birthplace showing burnt timbers. Edward Wakeling Collection, 1990.

It is interesting to note that there is now a Nursery (but no Schoolroom) on the ground floor, with 'a small room adjoining and a passage to it'. There is a 'W.C.' upstairs in addition to the 'privies' in the yard. In between the bedrooms over the Drawing Room and the Dining Room is a 'Dressing Room'. The gig-house is now called the 'Carriage House' and a 'Coal place' with a trap door has been added.

The report goes on to list all that must be done to the Glebe Farmhouse and its outbuildings, also the responsibility of the incumbent. The total is estimated at £760..16s..0d.

Destroyed by fire

Local knowledge tells us that the Old Parsonage burnt down after the death of Reverend Spencer, 'while it was vacant for a short time.'[65] Perhaps the poor state of repair was the result of this fire and the subsequent abandonment of the building. Alternatively, it may never have suffered a fire. Interestingly, the Bishop's report mentions work to be done at the Glebe Farm on a pig-stye and some other buildings 'which were burnt down some years ago'. There is no other reference to a fire. However, a picture taken when the well-head was first revealed in 1990 does show some burnt timbers.

Sir Gilbert Greenall comes to the rescue

In 1885 the [remains of the] house with its gardens and paddock, as well as the Glebe Farmhouse and land were sold by the Diocesan Commissioners, at £1,303..18s..0d', the purchaser again being Gilbert Greenall, now 'Sir Gilbert', who received a baronetcy from Queen Victoria in 1876 for his services to politics.[66] He was then seventy-nine and well-known as a benefactor, although still a serving MP. The new Vicar, Thomas Whitley, was his cousin, part of the Greenall Whitley Brewery family. Perhaps it had been difficult to find a minister willing to take over the parish without a vicarage. Certainly Reverend Thomas Whitley wrote at the time that he had taken on the living 'under exceptional circumstances and cannot hope to be there long.'[67]

Left: Farmer at well head, Birthplace site. Chester Life, 1948. Right: Birthplace monument, set up in 1974 by Daresbury Lewis Carroll Society (since repositioned).

The sale price took into account 'Dilapidations' valued at £760..16s..0d – the exact sum owed by the executors of Reverend Spencer as calculated in August 1884. Reverend Thomas Whitley, who took office in that month, tells us that the purchase was a generous act on the part of Sir Gilbert, 'for the benefit of the living.'[68]

As noted above, even forty years after its erection, the minister, the parish and the Dean and Chapter of Christ Church all knew that the Parsonage had been built in the wrong place, but since nobody was interested in buying the property, they had no way of resolving the problem. Perhaps Sir Gilbert's offer to buy it and make it part of his Walton Estate was the perfect answer. A newspaper article printed on Lewis Carroll's centenary, Wednesday January 27th 1932 states: 'It was pulled down when the patronage of the living changed hands.'[69]

Nothing remained but the well-head

By the time the OS map of 1898 was printed, the site had disappeared in the southern field.[70] The well-head was all that remained – and this is still visible in a photograph taken in 1948.[71]

'The Birthplace'

The site was first marked with a permanent monument on 27th January (Lewis Carroll's birthday) 1974. A bronze plaque, mounted on a stone plinth, stated: 'On this spot stood the parsonage in which Charles Lutwidge Dodgson (Lewis Carroll) was born on the 27th January 1832'. Members of the Daresbury Lewis Carroll Society (founded in 1970) were worried that: "it was soon going to be very difficult to find anyone who could lead you by the hand and say 'this is where the parsonage was'."[72] Also on the plaque is the excerpt already quoted from Lewis Carroll's poem 'Faces in the Fire'. The plinth and plaque have been repositioned since, but still stand on the Birthplace site.

What the trenches showed

 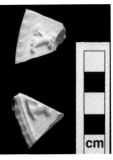 

In July 1990, Cheshire County Council carried out a brief archaeological dig on behalf of The Birthplace Trust. Eight trenches were dug and the remains of the well were found, although not quite in the position shown on the original plans of 1819. The four-week long excavation proved the ground floor plan of some of the rooms, although there was much evidence of robber activity. As noted above, a more extensive excavation would be required to provide greater detail.

It is interesting to note that some fragments of slate pencils and a few pieces of a child's ABC plate were found,[73] which could have been used as far back as the time of the Dodgsons.

Lewis Carroll's Daresbury Birthplace now

The site was acquired by the Lewis Carroll Birthplace Trust in 1992, with information panels being added in 1993. In 2001 the Lewis Carroll Centenary Wood was planted (now cared for by the Woodland Trust), with the idea of creating a path to join the two sites.[74] The Birthplace became the property of the National Trust in 2003. In 2010, decorative wrought ironwork, designed by Christine Wilcox-Baker, was put in place to delineate the foot-print of the building and the original front entrance.[75] The graceful ears of corn in its design refer back to Lewis Carroll's poem. New interpretation welcome panels and seating were installed in 2011.

Idyllic ...

Lewis Carroll had fond memories of his first eleven years as young Charlie Dodgson and, with the opening of the new All Saints Daresbury Lewis Carroll Centre in Spring 2012, visitors will be able to learn more about his birthplace. The sixteen years when it was home to a busy young family, eventually with ten children, as well as family, clerical, and local visitors, must surely have been the happiest time in the history of the Old Parsonage, Daresbury.

Left: Excavation finds. CHER Daresbury Parsonage Excavation Report, 1994.
Above: The Birthplace site, 2011, wrought ironwork designed by Christine Wilcox-Baker.

... But mis-placed

The two incumbents who followed Reverend Charles Dodgson had found it almost impossible to carry out their duties from the Parsonage built two miles from the church. It was not until, as suggested by both Reverend John Fawkes and Reverend William Spencer, the Vicar moved right into the village, that the problem was solved. In the 1891 census the Vicarage is shown in Chester Road, next to the Old Post Office. This house had belonged to Miss Felicia Williams, who ran a school for girls with her sister. It has since been demolished.

Above: Old Vicarage, Chester Road, since demolished. Moore and Daresbury Heritage Group

The New Vicarage, built in 1904-1906,[76] is opposite the church in Daresbury Lane. It is interesting to note that in August 1903, the Bounty Office was still causing delays:

Above and Right: The new Vicarage, Daresbury Lane, scale plan and elevation by the architects. CALS, DGB 5928/189.

'The Governors have just held their last Meeting before the recess, so that I cannot obtain their approval to the building till their November Meeting and I fear you cannot begin till they have approved the plans...'[77]

End notes

1 Letter in Christ Church Archives, Runcorn and Daresbury 14.12.1778
2 ibid 12.12.1808
3 ibid 13.10.1791
4 see note 2
5 Letter in Christ Church Archives, Runcorn and Daresbury, 05.05.1809
6 ibid 23.06.1812
7 ibid 08.03.1816
8 ibid 09.04.1816
9 ibid 18.05.1816
10 ibid 27.10.1816
11 ibid 27.11.1816
12 ibid 30.11.1816
13 ibid 20.12.1816
14 ibid 26.04.1817
15 ibid 26.04.1817
16 ibid 23.10.1818
17 ibid 03.12.1818
18 ibid 12.03.1819
19 ibid 20.04.1819
20 ibid 29.04.1819
21 ibid 07.06.1819
22 ibid 21.06.1819
23 ibid 01.07.1819
24 ibid 02.09.1819
25 Cheshire Archives & Local Studies, Plans Estimate and Specification for the building of Daresbury Parsonage, CCRO EEP 1137
26 ibid, 08.09.1819
27 ibid, 05.11.1819
28 Christ Church Archives, Runcorn and Daresbury, letter 18.11.1819
29 see note 25
30 Christ Church Archives, Runcorn and Daresbury, letter, 18.11.1819
31 ibid, 18.11.1819
32 ibid, 26.11.1820
33 ibid, 29.11.1819
34 see note 25, 14.12.1819
35 ibid, 26.12.1819
36 ibid, 12.02.1820
37 ibid, 05.04.1820
38 ibid, 28.04.1820
39 ibid, 08.05.1820
40 ibid, 29.06.1820
41 ibid, note in bundle
42 see note 25 or Daresbury Parsonage Excavation Report 1994, Cheshire Historic Environment Record, Document No.478 ISBN 0 906763 00 2
43 Ordnance Survey 1st Edition 25" to a mile, Cheshire Sheet XXV, 7
44 see note 42, page 29
45 Christ Church Archives, Runcorn and Daresbury, 23.01.1832
46 ibid 02.02.1832
47 National Census for 1841, Newton-by-

Daresbury, Parsonage House
48 Christ Church Archives, Runcorn and Daresbury, 05.12.1844
49 ibid 08.01.1845
50 Cheshire Maps online 'e-mapping Victorian Cheshire', Tithe Maps, Newton-by-Daresbury
51 National Census 1851, Newton-by-Daresbury
52 see note 53 below
53 Christ Church Archives, Runcorn and Daresbury, January 1857
54 ibid 01.08.1857
55 Churchwarden's Tribute *Lewis Carroll, A Biography* by Morton N Cohen, Papermac (Macmillan Publications Ltd), 1995, p 8
56 Christ Church Archives, Runcorn and Daresbury, 04.11.18
57 *The Life and Letters of Lewis Carroll* by S D Collingwood, 1898
58 Edward Wakeling, verbal communication
59 See note 24
60 Christ Church Archives, Runcorn and Daresbury, 05.04.1861
61 ibid 03.05.1861
62 Cheshire Archives and Local Studies, Bishop's Register, Book 27, p 187
63 Cheshire Archives and Local Studies: Dilapidations 1884-1905 EDP/101/3
64 Cheshire Archives and Local Studies: Index of Clergy EDA 20/4104/1
65 All Saints Daresbury, Notes by Edna de Prez, 1970 (also quoted in CHER Daresbury Parsonage Excavation Report, 1990)
66 *A Brewer's Tale* by J Norman Slater, pub. City Press Services for Greenall Whitley & Co.Ltd, 1980, p 135
67 Christ Church Archives, Runcorn and Daresbury, 22.11.1888
68 ibid
69 From a newspaper article, title: 'Birthplace of Lewis Carroll, The Old World Village of Daresbury and its links with Alice in Wonderland', signed 'L.W.T.' in the collection of Edna de Prez. Liverpool (?) Mercury, 27.01.1932
70 Ordnance Survey 2nd Edition, 25" to a mile, XXV, 7
71 Cheshire Life, December 1948, p 21
72 Warrington Guardian, January 1974, held in Warrington Library
73 CHER Daresbury Parsonage Excavation Report, 1994
74 *Lewis Carroll Centenary Memorial*, Joakim A Skovgaard, 2006
75 Funded by The National Trust
76 Cheshire Archives and Local Studies, P66/3339/3/10
77 Cheshire Archives and Local Studies, DGB 5928/189

1778	Revd Joseph Blackburn starts fund to build a parsonage house for Daresbury. CCA
1787	Death of Joseph Blackburn, parish goes to Revd Joseph Scott. Sells timber for house-fund. CCA
1808	More timber sold for house-fund. CCA
1809	Revd Joseph Scott has £300-£400 and starts looking for a suitable site to build on. CCA
1816	(Mar) General Heron and Sir Richard Brooke refuse to give up any land for a parsonage. CCA
	(Oct) General Heron agrees to exchange or sell a site in Hatton for a piece of the Glebe Land. CCA
	(Dec) The surveyor, Mr Thomas Wedge, will carry out a valuation. CCA
1817	(Apr) Mr Wedge refuses exchange – poor land in Hatton, good land in Newton-by-Daresbury. CCA
1818	(Oct) Revd Joseph Scott has died, his assistant curate applies for his position. CCA
1819	(Mar) Revd Robert Fletcher appointed to Daresbury, suggests building on Glebe Land. CCA
	(Jun) Mr Fletcher sends estimate and plan for Glebeland site to Dean & Chapter at Christ Church. Mr Blackburn informed house to go ahead, money he holds is required. CCA
	(Jul) Christ Church approve plans, write to office of Queen Anne's Bounty to augment funds. CCA
	(Sep) Bounty Office say should not have started building. Builder wants 50% payment (£637..10s). Mr Fletcher advances £300 from own funds. CCA
	(Nov) Christ Church send another £337..10s. Bounty Office approve funding but need plan etc. CCA
	(Dec) Mr Fletcher sends Plan & Estimate to Bounty Office. Too late & no affidavit from surveyor. CALS
1820	(Feb) Mr Fletcher sends affidavit from surveyor & statement from builder. Bounty Office complain not properly sworn. Will put before Board but need properly sworn affidavit. CALS
	(Apr) Mr Fletcher sends new affidavit. Writes to Christ Church for more money, builder finished. CALS
	(May) Payment finally agreed by Bounty Office – not yet sent. CALS
	(Jun) Mr Fletcher chases Christ Church for money (eventually paid in July). CALS
1827	Death of Mr Fletcher. Appointment of Revd Charles Dodgson. CCA
1841	National Census shows 22 people staying in Parsonage House overnight. NC
1843	Mr Dodgson moves on to Croft-on-Tees. Revd John Fawkes takes position. CCA
1851	National Census shows Mr Fawkes lodging in Daresbury village (not in Parsonage). NC
1857	Revd William H Spencer new incumbent. CCA
1859	(Autumn/Spring 1860) Lewis Carroll takes photos of Parsonage when visiting birthplace. NMM
1861	National Census shows Mr Spencer and young wife living in Parsonage. NC
1862	Christ Church sells patronage of Daresbury Chapelry to Gilbert Greenall, landowner of much of parish. Money invested in Queen Anne's Bounty Fund. CCA
1871	National Census shows Mr Spencer and family living in Parsonage House. NC
1880	All Saints Daresbury becomes separate parish in Chester Diocese, no longer under authority of Christ Church. (Daresbury, Hatton, Keckwick, Preston, Newton, parts of Moore & Acton Grange). CALS
1881	Nat. Census shows Revd Spencer and family living in 'the Vicarage' in Newton-by-Daresbury. NC
1883	Revd Spencer dies Oct 16th. Churchwardens given 'sequestration order' to enable them to run parish until next vicar is appointed. CALS
1884	(Aug) Dilapidation report on Parsonage shows much damage, repair costs £760..16s. CALS
	(Aug) Revd Thomas Whitley takes over as incumbent 'under extraordinary circumstances', lives in village of Daresbury. Could this refer to fire at Parsonage? [No record of fire discovered.] CALS
1885	Sir Gilbert Greenall buys land and buildings at Newton-by-Daresbury & Lower Whitley. Sum takes into account value of 'dilapidations'. Money held for new vicarage in Bounty Fund. CALS
1891	Nat. Census shows Revd Thomas Whitley and family living in The Vicarage, Chester Road. NC
1904	Foundation stone of New Vicarage is laid in Daresbury Lane, opposite church. CALS
1906	Bounty Office pays over last instalment of monies held in trust for All Saints, Daresbury. CALS
1974	Birthplace marked with bronze plaque on stone plinth by Daresbury Lewis Carroll Society. CL
1990	Cheshire County Council undertake trial excavation of Old Parsonage site. CHER
1992	Site acquired by Lewis Carroll Birthplace Trust. LCCM
1993	First interpretation panels mounted by Lewis Carroll Birthplace Trust. LCCM
2001	Lewis Carroll Centenary Wood planted, with memorial stone, near to Birthplace Site. LCCM
2003	National Trust take over Lewis Carroll Birthplace Site. LCCM
2011	New interpretation panels displayed at Birthplace Site by National Trust. NT
2012	Official opening of new Lewis Carroll Centre in All Saints Church, Daresbury.

ASD	All Saints Daresbury	**NC**	National Census	**CHER**	Cheshire Historic Environment Record
CCA	Christ Church Archives	**CL**	Cheshire Life	**LCCM**	Lewis Carroll Centenary Memorial
CALS	Cheshire Archives and Local Studies	**NT**	National Trust	**NMM**	National Media Museum, Bradford

Glossary

Advowson the legal right of the patron (see right) to appoint or recommend a priest to a Church of England (C of E) parish.

Affidavit personal statement made under oath and signed in presence of person with legal authority, who also signs it.

Bequest a gift of property or money, often for some particular purpose, left by will.

Chamber bedroom.

Chapelry the district legally assigned to and served by an Anglican chapel, in this case a group of townships within a larger parish.

Chimney-piece decorative construction around a fireplace, often with shelf above.

Cistern a tank for catching and storing rainwater.

Common flags stone slabs for flooring.

Copper copper bowl for boiling water in.

Cornice moulding at top of walls of room, between the walls and ceiling.

Corn and Hay Tithe yearly payment due on yield of corn and hay.

Cow Tithe yearly payment due on cows owned, also known as Easter Roll in Daresbury.

Curate clergyman, generally assisting in a parish, but see also perpetual curate.

Daresbury Delph former stone quarry in Daresbury (pronounced 'Darsbury').

Deal boards floorboards, from kind of pine or fir.

Dean and Chapter governing body of a cathedral, in this case, Christ Church, Oxford.

Diocesan Commissioners church authorities that administer regional areas, answerable to bishop.

Dodgson family name of Lewis Carroll, pronounced 'Dodson'.

Dust hole place where rubbish can be thrown, like a 'dustbin'.

Easter Roll yearly payment due at Easter time, in Daresbury's case the Milk Tithe.

Gig-house building in which to keep lightweight carriage or 'gig'.

Glebe Land land owned by the parish church, usually farmed to help support the incumbent.

Incumbent clergyman appointed to a particular living or benefice, in this case the chapelry of Daresbury.

Joice/joist horizontal load-bearing beam in floors, ceilings or roofs.

Lackerd/laquered varnished durable finish.

Lattis/Lattice window with small diagonal panes.

Living land and money allowed to support C of E clergyman, in past sometimes included tithes paid by parishioners.

Minister of the church appointed to carry out particular duties and offer spiritual guidance.

Newel end post at foot of staircase.

Pantry/pantries walk-in cool store-room for food and dishes, off kitchen.

Parson the parish priest who receives the benefice or living.

Patron/patronage having the legal right to appoint a parish priest or to recommend him to the bishop.

Perpetual curate C of E clergyman in charge of a chapelry, usually with a low income.

Privy/privies basic toilet facilities in a small outdoor shed, in this case also called 'the necessaries'.

Pulley/pullies circular pull-cord mechanism for raising or lowering sash windows.

Queen Anne's Bounty fund set up in 1704 during Queen Anne's reign, granting money under strict conditions to improve the living in a C of E parish.

Rapper door knocker, the thing that raps on the door.

Rector priest or church body having right to the income from the parish church, in this case the Dean and Chapter of Christ Church.

Sash windows windows opened or closed by sliding one frame of glass panels up or down over another with a hidden pull cord mechanism.

Shippon cow-shed

Slop stone slab of stone with slightly raised edges set at a slight angle so that water (and 'slops') can drain away, (sink).

Small Tithes yearly payment made by parisioners for produce, eg sheep, pigs, geese.

Stantions/Stanchions vertical supporting bars.

Stipend fixed and regular payment, such as a salary for services rendered or an allowance, in this case the parson's income.

Stuco/stucco plaster or cement finish, in this case for interior walls.

Tap room bar selling alcoholic drinks.

Tithe a payment due on land or its produce, including animals, originally one tenth part of what was produced.

Township a subdivision of a parish, responsible for overseeing its own poor and its highways.

Toll/turnpike road roads maintained by scheme of payments or tolls paid to those responsible for their upkeep.

Vicar C of E parish priest, where parish assets belong to another body such as a cathedral, college or monastery.

WC water closet, toilet facilities.

Acknowledgements

Whilst I consulted many books and documents, there are a few people I would like to thank particularly for the help they gave me in the research I undertook:

Reverend Canon David Felix, Vicar of All Saints, Daresbury

Edward Wakeling, Lewis Carroll Consultant

Keith and Liz Wright of Daresbury Lewis Carroll Society

Judith Curthoys, Archivist, Christ Church, Oxford

The helpful staff of Cheshire Record Office and Warrington Library (Cheshire Archives and Local Studies, acknowledged in text as CALS). Particularly useful website http://maps.cheshire.gov.uk/tithemaps

Moya Watson, Cheshire Archaeology Planning Advisory Service

Rupert and Christine Willcox-Baker

Moore and Daresbury Heritage Group

Richard de Prez, son of the late Edna de Prez, former All Saints parishioner, who left copious notes.

I shall be interested to know if any more light can be thrown on the subject. I can be contacted by email at: pam@hussingtreedesigns.com

Pamela Harbutt
October 2011